# Getting Ideas

Jeff Gill

Vellerosus press!

First published November 2015 by Vellerosus Press, Conwy, UK.

ISBN 978-0-9934865-0-0

Cover and interior design by Jeff Gill.
Typeset in Legato and **Alegreya**.

Printed and bound by Blurb.

vellerosus.com
jqgill.com

For Christine. She knows where to find all the ideas.

IAN,

THANK YOU FOR BUILDING SUCH AN INSPIRATIONAL SCHOOL AND FOR BEING ABSOLUTELY STUFFED WITH IDEAS!

## Skipping introductions is a perfectly reasonable thing to do but I want you to read this one, so I made it short

Ideas are tricky. Some people have ideas all the time. Some people never seem to have any ideas. Some people have plenty of ideas but they're all the wrong ideas. I get paid to have good ideas and make them happen, so I've had to learn how to have ideas all the time. If I don't, my family might have to become beggars or go to work for the companies that make those ads that pop up when you are trying to watch a video.

Ideas are not just tricky. They are fun too. Fun should be shared. That's why I wrote this little book. What I'm going to tell you works for any kind of idea – a funny new way to draw a cat, how to land a spaceship on a comet after travelling 10 years to get there, how to cure an illness or how to make a crying baby happy.

Let's get started.

## What is an idea?

Ideas are tiny tiny weird creatures that fly around the universe hoping to slip into a head that will know what to do with them.[1] Here are some ideas magnified thousands of times. I haven't drawn any actual size ideas because they are so small they can slip through your hair and your skin and your skull as easily as you can slip between trees in the woods.

1    This is a lie. The truth is that ideas are tiny bits of electricity zapping...

6

There are millions and trillions and quadrillions[2] of ideas flying around bumping into each other and everything else all the time. We'll never run out of ideas because they are reusable. Most of them live forever. Also, when they bump into each other, sometimes they make a brand new little baby idea. Right now, there are so many ideas flying around that it's hard to not bump into 30 or 40 of them every time you move your head. Ideas are like those little flying insects that swarm above a stream on a hot summer day, except everywhere. Even so, some people still have problems finding them.

I wrote this little book to help you get new ideas more easily. The first thing you can do to get an idea is relax. You don't have to create an idea. The ideas are already out there. Your job is to be the kind of person that ideas like to fly into.

## How to be the kind of person that ideas like to fly into, part one: grow your head

If you can throw a stone and knock a can off a wall from 15 metres away, your friends are impressed at your stone throwing skills. It's hard to hit a small target from far away. You have to have very good aim. Ideas have terrible aim. They will try to fly into a head

---

... between your brain cells. The truth is interesting but it's not helpful when it comes to getting new ideas. The lie about ideas being tiny creatures is helpful. This book is full of helpful lies.

2 Quadrillion is a real number.

THIS,
BUT ONLY
ON THE
INSIDE.

and end up at the top of a pine tree. If you want a lot of ideas to fly into you, you should be a cliff. Millions of ideas hit cliffs every hour. The problem with cliffs is that they are too dumb to know what to do with ideas.

You, on the other hand, probably know exactly what to do with a good idea. Your problem is that you are a small target. You need to get bigger. Actually, only your head needs to get bigger. There's no point in growing your stomach. It's almost as dumb as a cliff. You don't have to grow the outside of your head either, just the inside. The best way to grow your head is to stuff it full of knowledge. Learn something every chance you get. Be curious.

Not long ago I was sitting in a coffee shop drinking coffee and looking out the window. I saw a man walking along the pavement with seven brand new floor brushes. Seven! Why did he need seven floor brushes? I was curious. I'm still curious. I wish I had run out of the shop and said to the man, 'Excuse me, sir. Would you mind telling me why you are carrying seven brand new floor brushes?' Can you imagine how many ideas would have flown into my head if I had learned what his seven brushes were for? My guess is guess 18½.[3]

Some people think you should avoid knowledge when you are trying to have ideas. These people like to quote Albert Einstein who said, 'Imagination is more important than knowledge.' They seem to forget that Einstein didn't say knowledge wasn't important. People are more important than food but the only people who truly believe that food isn't important end up dead in about six weeks. Imagination is more important than knowledge

---

3   There are lots of half ideas flopping around hoping they'll smash into another half idea and become a whole idea.

but knowledge is the food of imagination. Einstein couldn't have changed the science of physics forever if all he had was funny hair and imagination. First he had to feed his imagination with lots and lots of knowledge about gravity and the speed of light and rubber sheets.

If you want to discover new ideas, this is the one time when it's okay to be bigheaded. Ideas need a big target. Here are some ways to turn your head into a big idea target:

- Be curious.
- Pay attention in school. Even the boring bits might be tasty to ideas.
- Ask questions and listen to the answers.
- Really listen when people talk to you. Don't just wait for your turn to talk.
- Read. Read books. Read articles. Read cereal packets and shampoo bottles. Read online and off paper. Especially read things that people have taken the time to write well.
- Watch videos and films that teach you amazing things and tell you incredible stories.

Once you have some knowledge in your head – of course you already do! – try mixing it up a little. Ideas love different kinds of knowledge swirled together. What happens when you mix history with cupcakes or comics with styling your hair? Ideas happen. They happen to fly right into your head.

## How to be the kind of person that ideas like to fly into, part two: be silly

How many times have you been told, 'Don't be silly!'? All day long parents tell their children to not be silly. Teachers tell their pupils, 'Don't be silly!' You might even have friends who are always telling you, 'Don't be silly!'[4] They're right, of course. Sometimes. Life gives you quite a few situations where silliness is not helpful.

You should not be silly when you are taking an exam, even if the exam is a pointless waste of time dreamed up by the Government Education Minister who woke up one morning to find his favourite slippers chewed by the dog, his coffee too weak and someone on Twitter calling him a rude word so he went into his office and said to his assistant, 'This nation is in a terrible state – dogs chewing slippers, weak coffee and morons on the internet being rude to Important People. We're going to fix it, Alastair.'

'How are we going to do that, Sir?' said his assistant Alastair.

'We're going to write an exam to make sure the children of Our Great Nation know how to behave. Question one: What is the proper location for a dog? Write that down, Alastair.'

'I've written it, Sir. What's the answer, Sir?'

---

4   You could be right in the middle of a perfectly reasonable experiment with some yoghurt and a pair of socks when your oh-so-grown-up (by which I mean boring) friend grabs the yoghurt pot and says with all capital letters, 'DON'T BE SILLY!' My advice in a situation like that is to make sure you use your boring friend's socks for your experiment.

'Answer: The proper location for a dog is in the garden away from all slippers. [2 points]'

And so on.

Before long, you and all the other pupils in the country are taking the Education Minister's new exam. You know it is pointless. Your teachers know it is pointless. In his heart, even the Minister knows it is pointless. But it's too late because all the universities have decided that they won't let you learn anything from them unless you've scored at least a B on the Education Minister's pointless exam. It's pointless but you still need to be serious.

MR TOADYPANTS IS NOT AMUSED.

Another time to be serious is when you are flying an aeroplane full of babies home to see their mothers and one of the engines has just quit and the flight attendants have run out of wipes to clean up all the baby sick and stinky bottoms.

Another time to be serious is when conversing with a frog. Frogs may look silly but I have been on four continents and I have never met a frog who wasn't Entirely Serious At All Times.

BUT – and this is an enormous but – when you are hoping for a new idea, it is very very very very important to be not serious,

SOUTH AMERICAN
ENORMOUS
BUT-TAILED
BUSTARD

by which I mean, to be silly. Ideas love silly people. I'll give you an example. If you told your mum that you had whipped up a batch of disgusting and poisonous bacteria soup and thought you might drink a mugful before bed, she would say, 'Don't be silly. You'll make yourself sick.' BUT – the same huge but as before – drinking disgusting bacteria soup is exactly what Dr Barry Marshall did in 1984. He did it to prove his theory that sores inside your stomach called ulcers are caused by bacteria and not by stress. Until Barry Marshall drank his disgusting soup and gave himself an ulcer and then cured his ulcer with antibiotics, everyone thought ulcers were caused by stress. Today most ulcers can be easily cured by taking some antibiotic medicine, all because of Barry Marshall being silly.

When a new idea comes along, the easiest thing to do is throw it out. New ideas seem silly and useless but that's only because no one has used them before. Imagine if French farmer and astrophysicist Léon LeFarteaux had given up on his silly idea for super windy beans like everyone told him to. We'd all still be stuck on Earth and there would be no such thing as cheap holidays to Jupiter. I hope that you're brave enough to be silly like Barry Marshall and Léon LeFarteaux.

A good way to get started being silly is by making silly faces at yourself in the mirror. Blowing bubbles in your milk with a straw is good too. Sometimes when a song comes on the radio while I'm driving, I like to sing along with a funny voice as loud as I can. Whenever I think of a dumb joke, I tell it to my children. They think I just like dumb jokes. The truth is that I'm being silly

so that new ideas will notice me and land in my head.[5] There are literally[6] millions of ways to be silly. Remember when you used to lather up your hair with shampoo and then sculpt it into funny shapes? There's no reason why you shouldn't start doing that again. Try being silly at least twice every day and I bet you'll start having many more ideas visit your head.

5   I also like dumb jokes.

6   Many times when people say 'literally' they mean 'not literally'. I literally mean that there are literally millions of ways to be silly.

## How to notice when an idea visits you

You already know that ideas are too small to be seen. Most of them are also soft as the dust that collects under your bed. You could be bombarded by six dozen ideas at once and never know it. People miss most of the ideas that enter their heads. The way to notice an idea is to pay attention to the tiny tickles of their wings as they flutter around in your brain. Here are some of the best ways I've found of paying attention.

Get away from your television and computer and games console and phone and tablet. It's almost impossible to have a new idea when you are stabbing and swiping at a screen to find out who's having a yummy snack or which kitten did a cute thing.

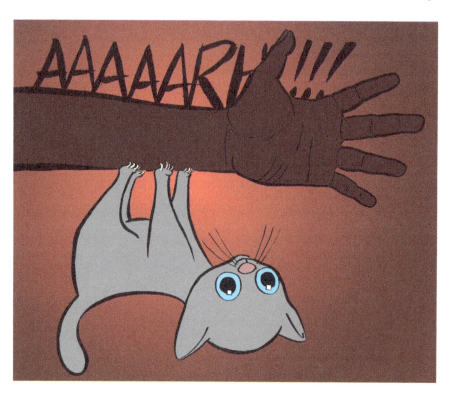

Once you have got away from the screens, let the ideas know that you are paying attention. 'Hello, ideas,' you could say, 'here I am with my head so full of knowledge it's the size of a beluga whale. I stuck a carrot in my ear too, because I'm silly. I'm ready for you! Please fly into my head.'

At this point what will probably happen is nothing. Ideas have bad aim. They are cheeky too. They hear what you say and decide to play a little game. They might avoid you completely to see if you'll get bored and go do something else. They might send a bunch of old ideas that you've had a million times before crashing into your head. The thing to do with old ideas is to notice them then set them to one side. A good way to do that is by writing down quick little notes – one or two words. You don't want old ideas getting in the way of the new ones.

When ideas are avoiding you completely, join in their game. Pretend like *you* are avoiding *them.* Pick up your pencil and do some doodling. Take a walk. Have a bath. Plop your nose in a pot of yoghurt. It doesn't matter what you do as long as it's something that leaves most of your brain free to notice ideas. Maybe give a casual whistle to show the ideas that you really don't care whether they fly into you or not. Soon the ideas will be so curious about whether or not you are ignoring them that they won't be able to help themselves and they will come crashing into your head like fat raindrops.

Waiting around for ideas might take a few minutes. It might take a few days. There's a good chance that you'll get bored while

you wait. You'll want to grab something with a screen to see if anything interesting is happening. Don't do it! Boredom is good. Boredom is your friend. The only reason William the Conquerer invented the car is that he was bored almost to death while riding his horse across the English Channel. Boredom is to ideas what lightbulbs are to moths. If you can work up some really strong boredom and manage to stick with it for a while, you'll soon find a flock of ideas flapping around inside your head.

When you notice one of those ideas in your mind, you'll say, 'Aha!' (or 'Eureka!', if you're in the bath[7]). You might get a tingle of joy that starts in your brain (or your toes) and spreads through your entire body. The idea in your head will squeal and laugh like a happy baby because ideas really do love to be noticed, especially by someone as clever as you. Imagine if you had been floating around since before the dinosaurs, bumping into cliffs and slugs and potatoes and people too busy worrying whether their last selfie was cute enough, and then you crashed into a head that was fizzing with information and curiosity and silliness. You would be thrilled. You might do a cartwheel of joy. You would certainly pop back out into the air and shout to your idea friends, 'Quick! Get in here! I've found the perfect place for an idea party.'

I have my best ideas when I am doodling, walking, taking a bath or washing the dishes. I was washing dishes when I had the

---

7   The reason why people say *eureka!* when they get an idea in the bath is that *eureka!* is what the great Greek mathematician Archimedes shouted when he had an idea about how to solve a problem for the king. *Eureka!* means 'I have found it' in Greek. When he found the idea or, to put it the way we're thinking about ideas in this book, when he noticed that the idea had found his head, he jumped out of the bath so excited that he forgot to put his clothes back on and ran, completely naked – I'm not making this up. I made some other things up but not this. He ran completely naked – bits in the breeze – from the city baths to his home so he could test his idea. His idea was a good one and he solved the king's problem. Eventually it became tradition to shout *eureka!* when you have an idea in the bath. Fortunately, running through town naked when you have an idea never caught on.

idea for this book. Ideas often arrive a while after you spend time filling your head with knowledge. I think ideas like to let information stew in your brain before they show up. Knowledge is food for ideas. Good food takes time to prepare. Dough needs time to rise before you bake it into bread. First, grow your head, then the ideas will come. All you have to do is pay attention.

## Multiply your idea attracting power with synergy

Synergy is the stuff that is released when two or three or six[8] idea-loving people spend time talking about ideas together. The word synergy comes from the words scent and energy.[9] Synergy actually means 'scented energy'.[10] When people who want ideas join with other people who also want ideas and they talk together about ideas an arc of energy forms between their brains. It's probably dark energy.[11] It's definitely scented energy. You can't smell it[12] but ideas can. If you could smell it, it would smell like cookies just out of the oven or freshly cut grass or petrol or whatever it is that smells nice to you. To ideas, synergy smells as good as knowledge tastes and as wonderful as silly looks. They can't keep away from it. The best thing about synergy is that ideas can smell it long before they notice your knowledge or see your silliness. Synergy gives you the ability to attract ideas from long distances.

Getting ideas with friends works in about the same way as getting ideas on your own. You talk about the thing that you need the idea for. You toss around some knowledge that you have

8   Or some other number less than 12.73.

9   No, it doesn't. It comes from the Greek word συνεργία which means 'to work together'.

10  That is a lie.

11  I am completely making this up. You should never let me teach your science class.

12  Because it's dark.

about the subject. You tell each other the old ideas that you've had before, to get them out of the way. All the time the synergy level between your brains is increasing. Then you throw in some silliness:

'What if we painted it bright pink?'

'Don't be silly! This is the most expensive and beautiful diamond in the world. If we painted it pink, it would look like plastic toy jewellery.'

'Annie, that's brilliant!'

'Is it?'

'Yes! We'll paint it pink and put it on a string with some beads. Your little sister can wear it. We'll walk to the rendezvous point in plain sight. The jewel thieves, terrorists and gangsters hidden outside your house won't suspect a thing.'

'Are you sure?'

'Yes! Because at the same time we'll send an empty armoured van escorted by men wearing dark suits and driving Range Rovers in the opposite direction.'

'Isn't that kind of an obvious diversion? It's been done in at least 50 action films.'

'Yeah, you're right. We need something better.'

At this point you and Annie are thinking so hard together that a giant cloud of lovely fragrant synergy is crackling and popping around her entire house. The ideas can't resist it. Within a couple of minutes, this happens:

'We could send a drone off in the wrong direction.'

'We don't have a drone.'

'We could call in an SAS hit squad.'

'The Chief of the Army said we aren't allowed to anymore.'

'Oh yeah. I forgot about that.'

'We could send up your mum's dressmakers dummy in your hot air balloon.'

'The gangsters would shoot a hundred holes in the balloon before it was half-inflated.'

And so on, until Annie says, 'My friend Bryony is a gymnast. She could do flips and jumps over the back fence into Mrs Croker's and through all the back gardens.'

'Perfect! We'll give her a bulletproof vest and a padlocked bum bag. Tell her to wear black. Let's do the armoured van too. Just to be sure.'

Boom. Diamond delivered. Disaster averted. All because ideas love scented energy.

Synergy doesn't automatically happen with any group of people. If you want an idea for a play you're writing about Irena Sendler[13] but your friend is obsessed with the pointless-celebrity-of-the-week's Amazing New Hairstyle, synergy will stay locked away. Or, if your friend wants to build a ginormous Lego robot but all you can think about is lunch, no synergy. You're not likely to produce any synergy with a friend who has no interest in ideas. You might be able to generate some synergy with a person you dislike, if you have been forced to work together by an apocalyptic alien invasion or your science teacher. It probably won't be fun synergy though. The most powerful, sweetest smelling synergy happens when you and a friend both love ideas, both want the same kind of idea and both are not afraid to be silly. I hope you have a friend like that.[14]

## What to do with a new idea

Here's a problem: you have a leaky head. I don't just mean dribble, snot and earwax. Ideas can fly out of your head as easily as they fly in. And they will fly out unless you do something to make them stay. The simplest thing is to do your idea as soon as it arrives. I was once being chased by an angry T. rex (a dinosaur,

---

13 Do write a play about Irena Sendler because she is one of the greatest heroes of the 20th century. Don't name your play *Life in a Jar* because that name for a play about Irena Sendler is already taken.

14 You can even generate synergy with your parents if they haven't forgotten how to be silly.

not Marc Bolan[15]) and I had the idea to turn round, run underneath it, then climb up its tail and onto its back and ride it like I was a Jurassic cowboy. Instead of trying that idea I decided to do some swerving back and forth and hiding under ferns. While I was doing the swerving and hiding, the cowboy idea slipped out of my head, which was unfortunate because the swerving and hiding didn't work. After a couple minutes the T. rex caught me and now I'm dead.

15 In the 1970s Marc Bolan had a band called T. Rex. They were very popular. You might think that a band called T. Rex would would feature lots of roaring and crunchy guitars. In fact, Marc Bolan liked to wear feathers and make-up and play bouncy fun tunes. The words for his songs seem like they drifted...

Sometimes you can't do an idea the moment you think of it, so you need to make it feel welcome and comfortable until you have time to try it out. Remember when you imagined flying an aeroplane full of babies home to see their mothers and one of the engines has just quit and the flight attendants have run out of wipes to clean up all the baby sick and stinky bottoms? Now imagine that while you're flying the plane you have an idea for how to make colour-changing candy floss. I don't think you should try to make candy floss in the cockpit of the plane. But you should make sure the idea sticks around until you land. You could ask for help. You could turn on the Tannoy and say, 'This is your captain speaking. I know this is a tense situation. Babies, your jammies

... up the rabbit hole from Wonderland in a happy jumble that didn't see a reason to get organised. I would give you an example of some T. Rex lyrics but you have to get permission and maybe pay someone some money if you want to quote song lyrics in books. Instead of bothering with all that, I wrote some T. Rex style lyrics to give you an idea of what they're like:

*He has gunk in his teeth*
*And his name is Keith*
*Ah ah ah*
*He has gunk in his teeth*
*And his name is Keith*
*Ah ah ah*
*I'd like to clean up his mouth*
*But my hand's made of tuna*
*Ah ah ah*

are covered in sick and your bottoms are smelly and you want your mummies. Flight attendants, you're having the worst flight of your lives back there. I'm doing everything I can to get us all home safe and sound. But for right now, could you try and remember something for me? I've had the most tremendous idea for how to make colour-changing candy floss and I don't want to lose it. When we land I'd like you to remind me of three things. The first is candy floss. The second is radioactive waste. The third is seagulls. If you can do that for me, I promise you'll be the first people in the world to try my amazing new confection. Thank you. I'm going to get back to flying now. We seem to be losing altitude rather quickly.'

When you have an idea you can't do immediately, you may not have a handy plane full of people to help you remember it, so you'll have to make it stay some other way. You could write it in a notebook or type a reminder on your tablet or phone. Recording ideas is an excellent use for your mobile device. I was on a walk when I had the idea to write that you have a leaky head. I typed this note on my phone to help me remember:

*You have a leaky head*
*Not just dribble and snot and earwax*

You could also draw a quick reminder picture. If you don't have any way to record the idea, just repeat it over and over to yourself until you are sure it will stick around until you get to a pencil and some paper.

Some ideas are babies when they flutter into your head. Trying to use a baby idea as soon as you get it is like trying to do anything with an actual baby. The baby doesn't help out at all and you're stuck with a crying poopy mess. Baby ideas haven't grown enough to be useful. They need time to eat the information in your lovely warm brain. They need time to play with other ideas. They need time for you to figure out what they are for.

Here are two examples from the world of creepy crawlies. Maggots[16] seem entirely useless but it turns out that they are the best way to clean dead infected flesh from wounds. They eat it! Hospitals use maggots to save lives.[17] Silkworms are really boring. Their favourite thing to talk about is pickled eggs. They never want to go out ice skating or to see a movie. They make terrible friends, but it turns out that they are extremely good at making silk which is used to make lovely clothes and sheets.

Your baby idea might seem entirely useless. Give it a nice warm space in your brain and feed it some interesting thoughts anyway. It might grow up to save lives or change the world of fashion. You never know with ideas, so try not to lose them. Write or draw or type them as soon as they visit your brain.

## Bad reasons to not have new ideas

**1. You're in high school.** A lot of high school is about passing your exams. Exams are hard work. You have to learn fact after fact after fact after fact. You have to learn theories and formulae and rules. While you are working hard at growing your brain with all that knowledge, it is easy to stop noticing ideas for a few years. Please don't! Remember, the point of knowledge is to grow your head so that ideas can easily find it.

16  Baby flies. Maggots look like grains of rice that have come alive, which is a fact you should definitely not mention next time your family is enjoying a nice takeway meal.

17  This is true.

Some people are convinced that the purpose of getting knowledge is to pass an exam or win a quiz. These poor people are about as clever as a cliff when it comes to new ideas. Treat them kindly but warily, like an elderly relative who has completely lost his mind and is usually sweet but sometimes throws his dinner at the cat. You enjoy his stories about when he was a boy but you wouldn't start a business with him or let him babysit your little brother. People who love knowledge but avoid ideas are like that. You should also be cautious about people who love ideas but avoid knowledge. These are the kind of people who believe advertisements on the telly and try to wallpaper the cat and start wars on purpose.

Interesting people never figure out how to stop getting ideas, even during exam season. Their teachers give them stern looks and their parents worry that they might be too silly. But interesting people carry on noticing the ideas that flit into their brain. The most interesting people notice their ideas and DO them.

**2. You have a terrible job.** Sometimes you have to do a job you hate in order to have the money you need to buy food and a place to live. Terrible jobs make you sad. Terrible jobs make you want to sit on the sofa and drink wine and watch the telly all evening. But being a grown up means that you are smart enough to not do what you want all the time. Even if a terrible job takes up 40 hours of your week, you still have 128 hours left for ideas. You need those ideas so you can escape from your terrible job.

**3. New ideas are dangerous.** Here are some ideas that were new once:

- Earth isn't the centre of the universe.
- Kings and queens should obey the law like everyone else.
- Women are not inferior to men.
- People should be treated equally no matter what colour their skin is.

These ideas seem obviously true to us but people have died for having them.

New ideas are dangerous because the people who have power rely on old ideas. If old ideas get replaced by new ideas, people with power might not have power anymore. In case you are wondering, power is nice to have. It usually comes with lots of money. People listen to what you have to say. You can have the things that you want. Power is so nice to have that it makes kind people turn cruel rather than give up their power. It makes clever people fight against new ideas rather than give up power. New ideas are often exciting to people without power and frightening to people with power.

The world changes when a brave person like you does something with a new idea. People are afraid of change but that's no reason to ignore your ideas. Be kind to the people who are afraid (even if they are cruel to you) and go right ahead with your new idea. There is a lot wrong with the world. Your ideas can help make it better.

**4. New ideas can be embarrassing.** New ideas aren't always right. Sometimes old ideas are better. If you have a new idea and it turns out to be wrong, you might be embarrassed. People might make fun of you. Your friends might not want to be around you.

Christopher Columbus had the idea that the Earth was round and that you could sail to East Asia and India by going west. He was right about the Earth being round but wrong about getting to Asia because North and South America are in the way. Embarrassing! Christopher Columbus could have been so embarrassed that he hid in the Americas forever. But he didn't. He went back to Spain and told everyone what he found. His discovery led to all kinds of things, good and bad. One of the best things is that the United States was founded so that burgers could be invented.

When a new idea takes you in the wrong direction, you might feel like giving up on ideas altogether. Instead of giving up, think about Christopher Columbus and tasty burgers. Being silly helps too. Silly people see the funny side of life, including the funny side of being embarrassed. The embarrassment might be worth it if you learn from what went wrong and improve your idea.

I'M SURE
I'LL LAUGH
ABOUT THIS
LATER.

# *What if you have an evil idea?*

I told you before that there are quadrillions of ideas flying around. Most bad ideas are actually good ideas that got lost and have bumped into the wrong head at the wrong time. Of course, some ideas are truly terrible. One example of a truly terrible idea is being cruel to someone because they are different from you. Another example is British baked beans.

You might be worried about having ideas in case you have a truly terrible idea. You might be worried that having a truly terrible idea makes you a truly terrible person. Don't. You're not. A good way to be sure that you are not truly terrible is that you are worried about it. Truly terrible people don't care at all about being terrible. Before a terrible person is born something goes terribly wrong with their growing brain. The part of the brain that cares about other people doesn't grow right. This happens to less than one percent of people. If you care about other people, you can't be a truly terrible person. Check once in a while to make sure you're not truly terrible person but don't waste a lot of time on it.

There is a good chance that while you are waiting for a new idea you will have a terrible idea. Sometimes when I'm standing on a high bridge or near the edge of a cliff I have this idea: JUMP! I didn't have the idea because I'm sad and want to die. I love being alive! My wife says that sometimes she has the idea of shoving her hand in the blender. Of course she never does it. It's a terrible idea. But people who pay attention to ideas get bad ideas sometimes. Don't worry about it. If an ugly or evil idea bumps into you, just tell it, 'No thanks. I don't need your type around here. I won't be cutting off my little brother's toes today.'[18]

You cannot control what ideas fly into your head. You can decide what to do with them. You are you and ideas are ideas. When you step in a big pile of poo, like elephant poo or whale poo, that doesn't mean you are a poo. It means you need to clean your shoe. In the same way, a nasty idea doesn't make you a nasty person. Hang on to the kind ideas. Send the nasty ones politely away. Maybe they are just lost.

18  Even this could be a good idea that got lost. Imagine that your little brother was caught in an invincible toe trap and there was a bloodthirsty rhinoceros running towards your brother because it was particularly fond of devouring tender little boys. Imagine all you had was a sharp knife and a few seconds to get back to your helicopter. In that situation the toe chopping idea is exactly what you want flying into your head.

# *Finally*

Here is a quick review of what I have told you about ideas:

- Ideas are tiny weird creatures looking for nice big heads full of tasty information.
- Grow your head with all the interesting information you can find, then mix it together.
- Ideas like silly people because silly people will try new things.
- Spend time away from screens so that you can notice ideas visiting you.
- Spend time creating synergy with your friends who love ideas.
- Be sure to write, type, memorise or – best of all – try out an idea as soon as it visits you.
- People are afraid of new ideas but you don't have to be.
- Having a horrible idea doesn't make you a horrible person. You didn't create the idea and you don't have to do it.
- Use the kind ideas and send the nasty ones away.

That's it. You'll notice that I didn't tell you to be super smart or super creative or super anything. You just have to do a few simple things[19] to make yourself attractive to ideas.

There is one more very important thing. When you have a good idea, remember to say thank you. You grew your head and

---

19  Simple isn't always the same thing as easy.

paid attention and ignored your fear, but all of that would have been for nothing if the idea hadn't come along when it did.

About 2000 years ago there was a king who was in a quarrel with the kingdom next door. He had the idea to make peace with the next door kingdom.[20] The people of the kingdom next door were on the losing side of the quarrel, so they thought the king's idea was wonderful. In fact, when he visited them to make a speech about his idea for peace, the audience started shouting, 'This is the voice of a god, not of a man!' Instead of saying thank you, the foolish king sat there and agreed with the crowd. 'I do sound quite a bit like a god,' he thought to himself. Next thing you know, the king was infested by flesh-eating worms and he died.[21]

I've never known anyone who was infested by flesh-eating worms but I do know that life goes a lot better if you say thank you, even if you can't see who or what you are thanking. Tell your ideas thank you.

Now...

---

20  It wasn't actually the king's idea. One of his trusted servants had the idea and gave it to him.

21  This story comes from the Bible. It's found in the book of Acts chapter 12 verses 19–23.

# Go be a silly bighead!

## About Jeff Gill (*that's me*)

My favourite things are drawing, designing, writing and inspiring other people to live creatively. My other favourite thing is hanging out with my family and friends. My other favourite things are comics, good stories with lots of action, and being outside. My

other favourite things are food and wine.

I would love to visit your school, office, clubhouse, tree house or secret headquarters and help you and your pupils, colleagues or friends find some ideas. You can contact me through my website, **jqgill.com**, where there is also lots to read and look at.

# Acknowledgements

Roald Dahl is one of my writing heroes. One of the last things he wrote was *Roald Dahl's Guide to Railway Safety*. I like it because it shows that books full of important information don't have to be dull. *Getting Ideas* is roughly modelled on Dahl's guide. I included 'tremendous' and 'fizzing' – two very Dahl-ish words – as a tribute to him. Maybe one day, if I keep practicing, I will be able to use them as well as he did.

Four people made this book possible. My wife Christine and daughter Freya gave me 9000[22] useful suggestions for improving what you just read. Angela Parvin read my manuscript, found mistakes and encouraged more than she knows. Caroline Wolstenholme also read my manuscript, found mistakes and supplied me with a transatlantic stream of creative inspiration. Thank you!

Many people have shaped my thinking about creativity, none more than Elizabeth Gilbert. A few of the others are my parents Dan and Dorie Gill, my friend Phil Rigotti, Terry Pratchett, Neil Gaiman, Steven Pressfield, Stephen King, Noel Gallagher, John Cleese, Rob Bell and Tommy Barnett.

---

22  I may have rounded up a little.

Lightning Source UK Ltd.
Milton Keynes UK
UKOW07f0652261115

263573UK00001B/4/P